T0361185

# THE INDUSTRIAL REVOLUTION

# THE INDUSTRIAL REVOLUTION

MARY BEGGS-HUMPHREYS, HUGH GREGOR AND
DARLOW HUMPHREYS

Routledge
Taylor & Francis Group

LONDON AND NEW YORK

First published in 1959

Reprinted in 2006 by
Routledge
2 Park Square, Milton Park, Abingdon, Oxon, OX14 4RN

*Routledge is an imprint of Taylor & Francis Group*

Transferred to Digital Print 2010

The publishers have made every effort to contact authors and copyright
holders of the works reprinted in the *Economic History* series. This has not
been possible in every case, however, and we would welcome
correspondence from those individuals or organisations we have been
unable to trace.

These reprints are taken from original copies of each book. In many cases
the condition of these originals is not perfect. The publisher has gone to
great lengths to ensure the quality of these reprints, but wishes to point out
that certain characteristics of the original copies will, of necessity, be
apparent in reprints thereof.

*British Library Cataloguing in Publication Data*
A CIP catalogue record for this book
is available from the British Library

The Industrial Revolution
ISBN 0-415-38222-X (volume)
ISBN 0-415-37837-0 (subset)
ISBN 0-415-28619-0 (set)

Routledge Library Editions: Economic History

# THE INDUSTRIAL REVOLUTION

Mary Beggs Humphreys
Hugh Gregor and Darlow Humphreys

London
GEORGE ALLEN & UNWIN
Boston          Sydney

First published in 1959
Second edition 1961
Third impression (minor alterations) 1965
Fourth impression 1968
Fifth Impression 1972
Third edition 1976
Second impression 1978

GEORGE ALLEN & UNWIN LTD
40 Museum Street, London WC1A 1LU

ISBN 0 04 942151 4

## Acknowledgements

Acknowledgements are due to the following for permission to reproduce illustrations:
BBC Publications, nos 23, 24; Bristol City Central Library, 36; Common Ground Ltd, 21, 31, 33; Industrial Heritage Trust, 22; Ironbridge Gorge Museum Trust, 6; Mansell Collection, 14, 26, 34, 35, 40, 43; Hugh McKnight Photography, 41; National Portrait Gallery, 27, 28, 29; Radio Times Hulton Picture Library, 2, 47, 48, 49, 50; Science Museum (Crown copyright), 9, 19, 20, 25, 39; Science Museum (Photographs), 5, 11, 37, 46; Vista Books, 8.

# Contents

# Illustrations

# Introduction
## Why we Talk of an Industrial Revolution

Between the mid-eighteenth and mid-nineteenth centuries Great Britain changed from a mainly agricultural country into a mainly industrial one. Because the change came about so quickly we can indeed describe it as a revolution.

This period of a hundred years might well be called 'the age of steam power'. Steam power was first developed, and then used in mills and factories, ships and railways, pumps and foundries. Between them steam, coal and iron transformed Britain's in-dustry, brought about a revolution in road, rail and sea transport, and led to the rapid growth of new industrial cities.

Both industry and Parliament were unprepared for such great changes in so short a time, and they often had to solve serious problems with little past experience to guide them.

In the pages that follow you can read more about the pioneers, their spectacular inventions, and the opposition they often faced.

# 1 The Story of Iron

Iron is the chief metal on which our civilisation today rests. Ninety-three per cent of all the metal we use is iron.

But iron is never found in its pure state in the earth. It is found as *iron ore*, that is iron mixed up with such substances as oxygen, sulphur, sand and perhaps clay. These are impurities not wanted in the finished iron, and the problem down the ages has been to find out how to separate the iron from these other substances. The answer is by *smelting* in a furnace.

## Smelting iron ore

Today we do this in huge *blast furnaces*, where iron ore, together with coke and limestone, is subjected to a great blast of air and heated up to 1800°C. (1525°C is the temperature at which iron liquefies.)

The carbon in the coke combines with the oxygen in the iron ore to form a gas. (See the illustration.) The limestone combines with the other impurities to form liquid slag which floats on top of the molten iron and is drawn off through the slag notch. The molten iron is drawn off through the tap hole into channels of sand called pig-iron beds. It will have absorbed some of the carbon from the coke and this iron is called *pig-iron* or *cast-iron*.

## Early ways of working with iron

*How early smiths made things from wrought-iron*
The first smiths built small furnaces not much more than a metre high, sometimes lined with clay, with a hole at the top and an air hole at the bottom. A charcoal fire was lit, and iron ore and charcoal were piled in. Air was blown through the hole at the bottom by bellows. Gradually the ore became soft. It never liquefied. It just became a soft lump or 'bloom'.

After about twelve hours the furnace was opened and the lump of iron taken out. But it was too brittle to be of much use (because, as we know now, it contained so much carbon and slag).

The smith hammered the soft iron to get rid of the impurities. He now had a metal that was pure and workable, one that could be made into tools, ploughshares, etc., at the blacksmith's forge. This is what we call *wrought-iron*, or worked-on iron.

*Smelting with charcoal*
As early as the fourteenth century in Britain, some ironmasters had found out how to reduce iron to a melted or molten state, though of course they were not able to produce a great enough heat to melt it completely. A temperature of 1525°C was needed for that.

By the seventeenth century some ironmasters had built furnaces 5 to 9 metres tall, often on the sides of a hill to make it easier to unload trucks of ore and charcoal into the top of the furnace. To increase the heat of the furnace there were great bellows 7 metres long, worked by waterwheels.

The molten iron now being obtained would be run off into sandy casts called 'pigs' (see illustration), or taken in ladles and poured into moulds. It was found that this pig-iron was of better quality than the old blooms, but it was still very brittle. It could be used for making ornamental shapes, but finer, stronger tools and weapons continued to be made of wrought-iron in the old way.

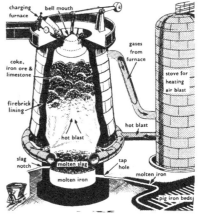

1. A modern blast furnace

2.  Making wrought-iron in the sixteenth century. The 'bloom-smith's' face is protected by a mask. In his right hand he has a bar with which he stirs the iron and beats out the cinder or impurities. The man with a wooden mallet is beating the 'bloom' after it has been taken out of the furnace. Next this 'bloom' is put on the anvil (bottom right) and beaten by a hammer which is driven by a waterwheel. Finally it is cut up into four or six pieces

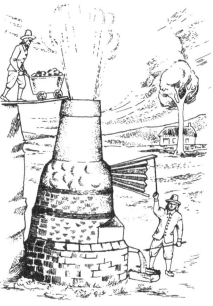

3.  A seventeenth-century furnace for making cast-iron

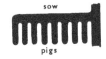

4.  How pig-iron got its name. When the molten iron was led off into sandy casts the process looked rather like a mother-pig feeding her piglets. Hence the term *sow* for the large cast, *pigs* for the smaller ones, and pig-iron for the molten cast-iron

### The dwindling forests

The chief centres of the early iron industry in Britain naturally grew up at places where there was iron ore to be found, forests for charcoal, and water for power—the Forest of Dean and the Sussex Weald were two of the best areas. The industry could also be found in Kent, Surrey, the West Midlands, North Lancashire and round Sheffield.

However, by the sixteenth century timber was in great demand for many other things besides making charcoal—shipbuilding, house-building, furniture and fuel. Indeed it was becoming so scarce that even the government was alarmed. In 1558 Queen Elizabeth's Parliament passed an Act forbidding the cutting down of trees for ironmaking in certain parts of England. In 1584 another Act forbade the building of any more ironworks in Surrey, Kent or Sussex. In 1674 all the royal ironworks in the

1. They made a clearing in the forest to obtain wood to build their stacks.
2. They made a circular hearth and erected a stake in its middle.
3. Lengths of wood were piled round the stake, some pieces put horizontally, some sloping to allow air to circulate.
4. The stake was removed and the hole left, to act as a chimney. Often other air holes were left around the bottom of the stack.
5. The stack was covered over with straw or brushwood and then with a layer of damp earth.
6. It was set alight with a torch and kept burning slowly until charcoal formed— that is, the wood changed into almost pure *carbon*. Then the top of the stack was closed off and it was left alone for five or six days.
7. When the stack was dismantled, the charcoal was sold to the iron workers for smelting iron ore. But it took six loads of wood to produce one load of charcoal, so the process used up a great deal of woodland.

Forest of Dean were closed.

By 1740, there were only fifty-nine furnaces left in England and pig-iron was being imported in ever-increasing quantities. It looked as though the British iron industry was doomed, unless some fuel other than charcoal could be found for smelting.

### Smelting with coke: the Darbys of Coalbrookdale

From time to time some ironmasters had tried to use *coal* instead of charcoal, but it choked the furnaces and the sulphur fumes ruined the iron. Yet as early as 1619, an ironmaster called *Dud Dudley* claimed to have used coal successfully. His idea was never adopted, and he blamed his failure on the opposition of jealous charcoal ironmakers and the English Civil War.

But the wars of the eighteenth century and the growing use of firearms and cannon, provided a growing market for iron.

Abraham Darby I (1678–1717) was the son of a Quaker locksmith. He set up a brass-making works at Baptist Mills near Bristol. Here he experimented with coke as fuel. Coke is made from coal. Abraham Darby covered piles of coal with clay and cinders, allowed in only a little air, and kept them smouldering for a week. The sulphur and other impurities were burnt off and the substance that remained con-

sisted mainly of carbon. Coke creates a better heat than charcoal and, being hard, is better able to stand a heavy load on top of it.

Abraham Darby moved to a small, derelict ironworks at Coalbrookdale in Shropshire and in 1709 he first smelted iron successfully with coke. Coalbrookdale had a number of advantages. Iron ore, coal and limestone could all be obtained from abundant local sources; the River Severn provided not only a source of power for bellows and hammers, but a convenient means of transporting finished iron goods to markets and customers.

In the early eighteenth century Coalbrookdale was producing kettles, pots, cauldrons and grates. Abraham Darby II (1711–63) took account of fresh needs and began to make cast-iron parts for the newly developed steam pumps and cannon. Abraham Darby III (1750–89) involved the family firm in ideas that were important in the later development of railways. In 1767, strips of cast-iron capping were put on top of wooden railway tracks for the first time to prevent them wearing out so quickly. In 1779 the firm designed and built a famous iron bridge across the Severn; it still exists today.

Coke smelting spread only slowly. It was more than a hundred years before it had completely replaced the charcoal-burning furnaces.

6. Abraham Darby's ironworks at Coalbrookdale, Shropshire. Notice in the foreground the cylinder on a cart that is pulled by a team of horses; and beyond the fence piles of coal being coked

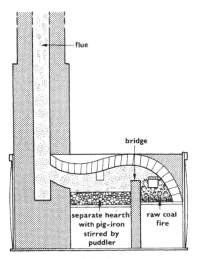

7. Henry Cort's puddling furnace

But coal for making coke was far more plentiful than wood for making charcoal. Because of this the iron industry gradually moved away from the forest areas of the south to the great coalfields—for example to South Wales, Derbyshire and Yorkshire.

| HOW SMELTING INCREASED IN ENGLAND AND WALES 1788–1826 | | | |
|---|---|---|---|
| Date | Number of furnaces | Furnaces using charcoal | Furnaces using coke |
| 1788 | 77 | 24 | 53 |
| 1826 | 266 | — | 266 |

### Wrought-iron: Henry Cort of Gosport

The increased production of pig-iron called for new ways of producing wrought-iron in larger quantities. Although several people were experimenting with new methods, it was Henry Cort who proved successful and patented his ideas in 1784.

*Puddling*
Cort's invention is best called 'puddling and roll-

8. Puddlers at work. The man on the left is stirring or *puddling* the molten iron with a long bar to expose all parts of the metal to the flames and burn out the carbon. When the bar gets too hot to hold he throws it into a trough of water behind him and takes a fresh one. The liquid metal becomes thick or spongy. The man on the right is taking it out in balls or *blooms* ready for rolling. The result is *wrought-iron*

ing'. Raw coal is burnt at one end of the furnace. The flue from which its smoke escapes is at the other end. In between is a separate sandy hearth in which the pig-iron is placed. The bridge built between the hearth and the fire makes the flames sweep down over the iron. The metal melts and is stirred by the puddler with his long 'rabble' or rod. Puddling gets rid of the carbon in the iron, which escapes in bubbles and little blue flames. It combines with the oxygen and passes out of the flue as a gas. The iron is then slightly cooled, rabbled into spongy balls, and taken by tongs to be hammered into bars.

### Rolling

Cort added another process. His puddled bars of iron were next reheated to white heat and *rolled*, perhaps two or three times in succession, to press out more impurities.

### Results

Cort's method was cheaper. Because the fuel never actually came into contact with the iron, he could use raw coal rather than coke or charcoal. Much more wrought-iron could be produced much more quickly; 15 tonnes of iron could now be produced in the same time that it had taken to produce 1 tonne.

Cort spent £20,000 on his foundries and supplied the naval dockyard at Portsmouth with wrought-iron items. But, like many inventors, he died in poverty, for the government never repaid him.

Two other improvements in the manufacture of iron need to be mentioned.

### Neilson's hot air blast (1828)

In 1828 James Neilson, manager of Glasgow Gas Works, proved that much fuel could be saved simply by heating the air coming into the blast furnace.

### Nasmyth's steam hammer (1839)

This overcame the difficulty of hammering great lengths of glowing metal on the forge. The problem had become very real when the engineer I. K. Brunel designed two very large passenger liners, the *Great Western* and the *Great Britain*. Their engines and engine shafts required forgings that were too large for the usual helve and tilt hammers.

## Steel

In the first half of the eighteenth century small amounts of steel were being made by the *cementation* process. Bars of wrought-iron were packed in clay vessels with charcoal, and then heated in a furnace for several days. But the carbon did not spread

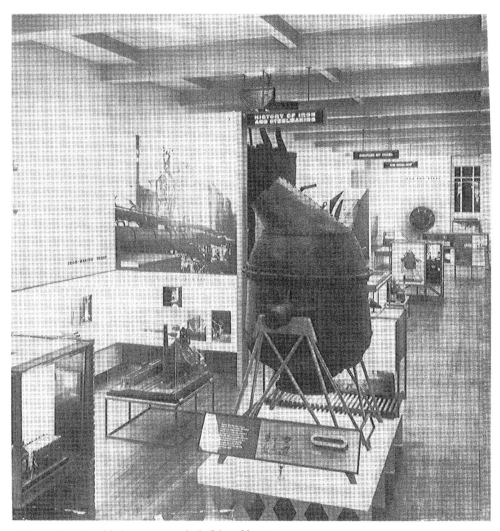

9. Henry Bessemer's original converter, now in the Science Museum

evenly through the iron and the steel produced in this way was of poor quality.

## Benjamin Huntsman: the crucible method

Benjamin Huntsman (1704–76) was a clockmaker from Doncaster. He needed high-class steel for the springs he used inside his clocks and watches. He reheated some of the poor quality steel in clay crucibles in a very hot fire until it was molten. The impurities were then skimmed off as slag and the carbon became more evenly spread through the metal. Huntsman's *crucible* method (1740) depended on developing a vessel capable of withstanding the great temperature needed, and on controlling the quantity of carbon. When Huntsman moved to Sheffield his ideas laid the foundation of that city's great steel industry.

## Bessemer: the converter

It was the inventor Henry Bessemer who succeeded in mass-producing steel. He was trying to develop a strong material from which to make cannon for use in the Crimean War (1854–6). He used an egg-shaped vessel called a *converter*. He melted iron in the converter and then literally blew out the impurities with an airblast coming up through holes in the

bottom of it. The exact amount of carbon was then added to create the steel he wanted.

## W. and F. Siemens: the open-hearth method

However, one impurity Bessemer could not get rid of was phosphorus and his converter of 1856 could use only phosphorus-free iron ore, which was imported from Spain or Sweden. The same limitation imposed itself on two brothers, W. and F. Siemens who in 1866 developed an alternative method of making steel—the *open-hearth* method. They used as a source of direct heat a mixture of hot air and hot gas beating down on a trough of metal.

## Thomas and Gilchrist: basic steel

Finally it was left to two cousins, Sydney Gilchrist Thomas and Percy Gilchrist, to solve the problem of phosphorus in British ores. They used limestone to absorb the phosphorus, and lined their vessels with a special substance called dolomite to withstand the slag formed by the limestone. Their '*basic*' method (1878) enabled the British steel industry to make better use of British ores.

Cheap, mass-produced steel could now be used for the construction of bridges, railways and ships, and foreign countries queued up to buy British.

# 2 The Story of Coal (1700–1870)

10.

Before 1750     1750 $4\frac{1}{4}$ million tonnes     1800 12 million tonnes     1850 56 million tonnes

Before 1700 very little coal was used except where people could easily dig it out from hillsides or from shallow pits. Then, with the growing shortage of wood and the growing demand for iron, the demand for coal increased. Deeper mines were dug, and they were extended further underground away from the shaft. The nineteenth century brought another steep rise in the demand for coal—for fuel, for power and for light. This was due to the growing use of steam engines, steam locomotives, steamships and the introduction of lighting by coal gas (1802). As mines became deeper and deeper to cope with this demand, so it became more and more difficult to extract the coal.

At the beginning of our period coal-mining was very much a family affair—husband, wife and children working as a team. Pits were shallow, and called *bell pits* because of their shape. The only tools available were pick, shovel and basket harnessed to muscles and sweat. Most of the coal would be distributed only locally over, perhaps, a ten-mile area. This was because coal was so difficult to transport in any quantity by packhorse or cart. Only if the mines were near the sea or a navigable river like the Severn, Wear, Tyne or Humber, was there a chance to supply a more distant market.

## Problems and dangers

### Conditions of work

Mining families might have to work at least twelve hours a day, and for much of the year they would never see daylight except on a Sunday. Long hours were acceptable in a family unit—people could take a rest period when they felt like it. But by the nineteenth century the situation had changed. Coal mines had become much larger, and were often privately owned by wealthy landowners. Many of these had little interest in the welfare of their workers.

### Haulage

Below ground coal was either carried to the bottom of the shaft in a wicker basket called a *corf* or hauled along on a wooden sled called a *tram*. The 'hewers' who cut the coal were usually the men; the 'putters' who dragged it from the coal-face to the shaft were the women and children. They had to work in low, narrow tunnels in almost total darkness, and in considerable danger, too. The heavy loads of coal often had to be carried up from one level to another using primitive ladders; one slip meant that the load would crash down onto anybody following behind.

By 1800 trams had first wooden wheels, then wooden rails to run on; now they could be pushed and pulled along the tunnels more easily. Children were harnessed to them with a girdle round their waist and a chain between their legs. They were expected to crawl along the tunnels like animals, very often doing permanent damage to their knees.

Small tunnels were less expensive to make, and it was more economical to use children to pull the trams than anything else. In the larger mines, however, pit ponies were introduced in the nineteenth century with children to lead them.

Above ground the coal might have to be transported several miles to a convenient river or canal.

11. Descent into a coal mine, early nineteenth century. Notice the wicker *corfs* that carried coal or people and the naked candle flame

Wooden and later metal rails, with the tubs of coal running on them, soon proved superior to the horse and cart. The weight of a string of tubs going downhill could be used to haul the empties back up again. Boulton and Watt steam engines spaced out at intervals gave an improved source of power, until finally the moving locomotive was used.

*Water*
As mines were made deeper, flooding became a serious problem. At first mine-owners tried using horses to turn a machine which hauled up buckets of water; but in many mines, however hard the horses worked, the water came in faster.

The first person to harness steam to pump out the water was *Thomas Savery*. In 1698 he patented a machine which he called 'The Miner's Friend'. Steam was passed from a boiler into an oval-shaped vessel, driving out the water it contained through a valve. The steam was then condensed by jets of cold water played onto the outside of the vessel. A vacuum was thus created inside, causing water to be sucked up through a pipe.

However, Savery's pump could raise water only about 18 metres for the boiler and the vessel could

not be worked at any great steam pressure or they would burst.

A more efficient and stronger pump was made by *Thomas Newcomen*, a Dartmouth blacksmith. He developed his pump in 1712 and it was designed originally for the Cornish tin mines. It worked at a rate of twelve strokes a minute, and could raise about 45 litres of water 45 metres at each stroke. However, it used vast amounts of coal, and there was none in Cornwall. Because the parts were almost home-made, they did not fit together very exactly and there was an unnecessary waste of power; and energy was wasted because the cylinder had first to be heated and then cooled. Despite its weak points, the Newcomen pump was widely used in coal mines.

Steam pumps continued to improve, but water disasters still occurred in the nineteenth century. Miners could easily break into a flooded or disused working. So in 1850 a law was passed which said that plans must be made and kept of all coal mines, showing the exact position of all the workings.

*The shaft*
Another possible source of danger in early coal

12. A series of pumps, one above the other, worked by a waterwheel at the surface. (Sixteenth century)

mines was the shaft. At first there was usually only one, used for both ventilation and haulage. Miners were lowered down and coal was pulled up first by a simple hand windlass, then by a *horse gin*. The advantage of this device was that it left the mouth of the shaft clear of obstructions. However, accidents in the shaft were common. If a rope broke, either a load of coal or a group of miners was sent crashing to the bottom of the shaft. Nor was the wooden lining of early shafts a guarantee against cave-ins. The introduction of Boulton and Watt engines for winding from 1784 onwards, the development of wire cable in 1829, and the use of iron shafting in the nineteenth century, all helped to make the shaft safer. This was vital: by now some mines were 120 metres deep.

## Gas

Coal mines were plagued by two types of gas: *choke damp* or carbon dioxide; and *fire damp* or methane. Choke damp killed by suffocation and could be dispersed by waving a piece of clothing around. Fire damp could cause underground explosions. In some pits a 'fireman', clad in damp sacks and a large hood, would be sent into a suspect area. He carried a long pole with a lighted candle at the end. He would explode the pocket of gas and then fall flat on his face to escape the blast.

But explosions occurred with increasing frequency. In 1719 a report from Gateshead stated that 'seventy men were all blown out of the pit by the violence of the blast, miserably maimed and mangled'. In 1866 there was an explosion at Oaks Colliery, Barnsley, and 334 people were killed.

The trouble was that the naked flames of the candles used by the miners below ground often caused fire-damp to explode. Many people tried to

13. How a Davy lamp worked

The flame was surrounded by a fine wire gauze. This let enough air pass through for the flame to burn. If bad gas was present in the air the flame turned blue and so warned the miner of danger. But the gauze prevented the heat from the flame from escaping and exploding any gas there might be outside. Exactly the same principle is used in garage heaters today.

Now miners usually have electric lamps fitted to their caps. Better ventilation plants and the use of electricity for lighting have made the Davy lamp unnecessary

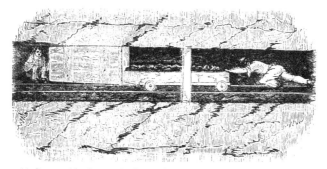

14. Boys working in an early nineteenth-century coal mine. The *trapper* has opened the door to let the other boy push the truck through

invent a 'safety lamp', including *George Stephenson*, famous later for his locomotive the Rocket. If you visit the Science Museum in London you can see models of their efforts. The most successful lamp, which gained a prize from the Royal Society and came to be used in most mines, was invented by *Sir Humphry Davy* in 1815.

### Ventilation

As mines went deeper, the problem of ventilation at the lower levels grew worse. Sometimes in the seventeenth century a man was employed to keep a great bellows working. A better solution to the problem was to have two shafts to the mine—one to suck fresh air in, the other to expel stale air and gases out. Often a furnace was placed towards the bottom of the second shaft. The heat created an upward draught to circulate the air round the workings.

Down in the mine the fresh air was guided around the tunnels by a system of wooden doors. These were opened and closed by small children called 'trappers', who sat crouched by their doors in total darkness to let the tubs of coal through.

### Dust

The air breathed by both miners and children was likely to be thick with dust. Crippling lung disease was one reason why, in 1844, the average life expectancy of a miner was reckoned to be forty-nine—ten years below the national average.

By the mid-nineteenth century mine-owners should have been applying the 1842 Mines Act, which forbade the use of women and girls underground, and boys under the age of nine.

The Miners Association was formed in 1841. The mineworkers were beginning to organise themselves in order to negotiate more effectively.

This combination of intervention by Parliament and self-help by the men was to bring about a slow but steady improvement in conditions.

# 3   The Revolution in Spinning and Weaving

### Old ways of spinning and weaving

To understand the inventions of the eighteenth century, we must first understand how the hand-spinners and hand-loom weavers worked in their homes.

1. The wool came from the sheep's back dirty and greasy. So first it had to be washed and *scoured*.
2. Then it was untangled by being drawn between wire brushes called *cards*. This is known as carding the wool—to get the fibres running in one direction.
3. Next came the spinning. Throughout medieval times and in some areas even into the eighteenth century, this was done with *distaff* and *spindle*. But those who learnt how to use the *spinning wheel* found they could make

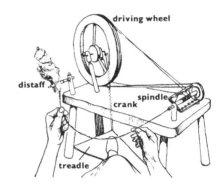

15. A seventeenth-century spinning wheel

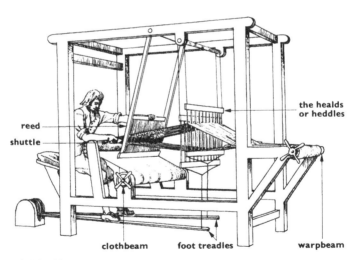

16. A hand loom

a finer and more consistent yarn. Spinning twisted the wool and drew it out.

4. Then the woollen yarn was dyed and woven into cloth on a hand-loom.
5. Next the cloth was fulled—washed with fuller's earth to remove grease and oil, and stretched on a frame to dry.
6. Finally it had to be dressed—the nap (the woolly fibres) was brushed up and then sheared smooth.

The woollen merchant or *clothier* was the man who organised other people to carry out each of these processes. They were carried on in peoples' homes, often in addition to their normal agricultural work. The women spun the yarn while the men were responsible for the weaving. This method of producing cloth was known as the *domestic system*. The processes were carried out by hand, and the workers set a pace that was convenient for themselves and their families. Simple though it was, this domestic system had so far met the country's needs well enough. Its main centres were the west country, East Anglia and Yorkshire.

There were, however, certain weaknesses in the system. The one-man loom could produce a cloth only as wide as the normal stretch of a man's arms, for the shuttle carrying the horizontal thread (the *weft*) was moved across the loom by hand. Secondly, the spinning wheel could produce only a single yarn at a time and could not easily keep up with the demands of the weaver.

## New inventions in spinning

### John Kay: the flying shuttle

In 1733 *John Kay* of Bury in Lancashire invented his *flying shuttle*, which was to cause a revolution in weaving. At each side of the loom he put a lever connected by a string. The weaver simply jerked this string with one hand, the lever struck the shuttle, and the shuttle was sent flying across the loom. It became possible to make a much wider cloth than before, and to produce four times as much. As a result, the spinners could not keep up with the demand for yarn, prices rose, and the blame was put on Kay and his invention. Twice his house was attacked, and in the end he had to flee to France.

17. A shuttle as used in Kay's flying shuttle

The older woollen industry was slow to adopt this and other new inventions because it was already doing so well. But the new cotton industry, then establishing itself in Lancashire, was eager for improved production methods. Moreover, since Britain was rapidly building an empire overseas, there was a growing market for cheap cotton cloth in tropical countries. Lancashire proved to be the ideal base for this cotton industry. The port of Liverpool imported the raw cotton and sent out the finished product. It was particularly well placed to accept raw cotton from America, and imports from there increased rapidly after the invention of the *cotton gin* in 1793 by *Eli Whitney*. This was a simple machine which plucked the seeds out of the cotton bolls picked by the plantation slaves much more quickly than they could do it by hand.

The damp climate of Lancashire and its even temperature suited the cotton fibres; in any other atmosphere the threads on the machines would be much more likely to break. The soft-water streams that flowed down from the Pennines were again ideal for processing the cotton fibre, and also provided a valuable source of water power. Lancashire was also fortunate in having ample supplies of coal underground so that the switch to steam power was easily made when it became necessary.

### James Hargreaves: the spinning jenny

Yarn continued to be scarce for about thirty years after the development of the flying shuttle. Then in 1765 *James Hargreaves* of Blackburn got the idea of making a machine which would turn many spindles at once. He named his machine after his daughter. It spun 16 threads at once and produced 120 times as much yarn as a single spinning wheel. Later improvements brought about a larger machine which could spin as many as 80 threads. Not surprisingly the hand-spinners thought their livelihood was threatened. Hargreaves had to face angry mobs of Blackburn spinners who broke into his house and smashed up his jennies.

### Richard Arkwright: the water frame

The spinning jenny produced a fine thread, but not a strong one. It was *Richard Arkwright* who developed a machine to spin a thread that was stronger.

Arkwright, who came from Preston in Lancashire, began life as a barber and wigmaker. However, he became interested in the manufacture of cotton, and in 1769 he patented a spinning machine that was driven by horse power, and set up a mill in

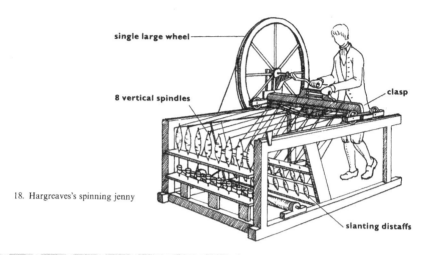

single large wheel

8 vertical spindles

clasp

18. Hargreaves's spinning jenny

slanting distaffs

19. Arkwright's first spinning frame
(Science Museum)

Nottingham. The following year, his partnership widened to include *Jedediah Strutt*, a hosier from Derby.

Strutt not only helped Arkwright to improve his machine but provided the money for further developments. In 1771, the partners decided to build a bigger and better mill and chose for its site a deep gorge of the River Derwent near the village of Cromford in Derbyshire. Now Arkwright could use water power to turn his machines.

Arkwright patented his *water frame* in 1775; it spun eight threads at once and produced a coarse but stronger yarn. But Arkwright had done much more than just produce a machine. He had produced a machine that could be worked by unskilled labour, that is women and children. His use of water power gave the machines the constant speed they needed to work at their best. When Arkwright built a new mill at Cromford in 1776 it was seven storeys high and 36 metres long. Here was the beginning of a new industrial system.

Despite hostility from domestic cotton spinners and opposition from his rivals, Arkwright prospered. He was knighted, became Sheriff of Derbyshire, and when he died in 1792 he was one of the wealthiest and most powerful businessmen in the country.

*Samuel Crompton: the mule*

From boyhood *Samuel Crompton* had seen hand-spinning and hand-weaving going on in his family home near Bolton in Lancashire. Meeting Arkwright and seeing how his machines used rollers to produce their coarse yarn gave Crompton an idea for a machine that would spin a yarn that was both fine and strong. But he did not perfect it until 1779.

Because Crompton's machine was a cross between the spinning jenny and the water frame, it was called the *mule*. It spun strong, fine yarn—even fine enough for making muslin. Crompton hoped to make a fortune out of his invention but he got nothing from the people who used it. In 1812 Parliament made him a grant of £5,000. But this was almost all swallowed up in paying his debts and he died in 1827 a poor man.

These great inventions had all been connected with spinning and by now the weavers could not possibly use all the yarn that was being produced. Another invention by a country parson was to alter all this.

## Weaving

*The Reverend Edmund Cartwright: the power loom*
One day when the Reverend Edmund Cartwright

20. Crompton's mule (Science Museum)

21. A power loom weaving shed, about 1830. Note the leather belts that drive the machines. At first the power came from a waterwheel, later from a steam engine

was on holiday in Derbyshire, he heard a spinner say that there would soon be so much yarn that hands would never be found to weave it. 'To this I replied,' wrote Cartwright, 'that Arkwright must set his wits to work and invent a weaving mill.' When the spinners said this was impossible, Cartwright said in that case he would do it himself. In 1785 he succeeded. Moreover, he was able to make use of a great new source of power. By 1785 *James Watt* had developed his steam engine and Cartwright used one of these engines to work his loom. Each loom could produce as much cloth as 200 hand-worked looms, and naturally there was great opposition from the hand-loom weavers.

Though others made fortunes, Cartwright made little for himself out of his invention. By 1793 he was so heavily in debt that he had to give up his new weaving and spinning mills at Doncaster. At last, in 1809, Parliament recognised his contribution to the prosperity of the country and voted him £10,000. Cartwright was then able to retire to a small farm.

### The plight of the workers

Workers like the hand-spinners and hand-loom

weavers hated the new machines, which forced down their rates of pay or put them out of work altogether. Sometimes, groups of them smashed up the new machines. For instance in 1811–12 the Luddite riots broke out in the northern counties and the Midlands. They were named after the mysterious *Ned Ludd* who was said to be organising the bands of machine-breakers. The government was forced to use spies and troops to break up the demonstrations. In 1812, hanging was made the penalty for frame-breaking, instead of fourteen years' transportation.

In the nineteenth century the application of steam power spread from the cotton to the woollen industry. The west country and East Anglia, not having enough coal, could not compete with Yorkshire, which became the centre of the woollen industry. By 1830 its yarn was spun by steam power, although much weaving was still done by hand. The number of power-looms it used increased only slowly—from 2,000 in 1835 to 9,000 in 1850.

In contrast almost all cotton spinning used steam power by 1830, and the total number of power-looms used jumped from 60,000 in 1830 to 250,000 in 1850. Other processes, too, such as fulling, bleaching, dyeing and printing, gradually became mechanised.

# 4 From Water Power to Steam Power

22. Under-shot waterwheels. Cheddleton flint mill, Staffs.

### The waterwheel

Giant waterwheels, made in very early times of wood and later of iron, powered the first machines of the Industrial Revolution. They were sited beside fast-flowing streams or rivers, and a weir or low dam was put across the stream to hold up the flow of water. This created a miniature reservoir from which a continuous flow of water could be directed to the waterwheel and then back to the main stream.

Waterwheels were designed to have water coming either over them (overshot wheels) or under them (undershot wheels). Whichever way they were turned, the shaft from the waterwheel passed through the wall of the watermill or factory and drove a series of lesser wheels and cogs to turn the machinery inside.

Waterwheels were a reliable source of power unless a long, dry summer cut down the volume of water flowing downstream. There was a growing need for a source of power that would be still more reliable, and steam pumps were developed, first by Savery, then by Newcomen, for pumping water out of mines.

### Steam power

*Newcomen's steam pump*
Newcomen's engine (1712) was known sometimes as a beam pump (because of its massive overhead beam), and sometimes as an atmospheric engine (because it used atmospheric pressure to push its piston down). Its main faults have been described already (page 15).

*James Watt: the steam engine*
James Watt was the son of a shipwright in Greenock, near Glasgow. At school he showed ability only at maths and drawing. His father wisely gave the boy a miniature forge and workbench, where he could make models of various sorts.

In 1754, Watt went to work in Glasgow, repairing astronomical instruments. He became apprenticed to a London watchmaker the following year, and then in 1757 he moved back to Glasgow University to work on mathematical instruments.

In 1763, a model of a Newcomen pump arrived on Watt's workbench for repair. He stripped it down to see how it worked and then, having mended it, he was dissatisfied with its performance. He puzzled over this for some time and came to the conclusion that this was because of the cooling of the cylinder after each upward stroke of the piston.

Watt's solution to the problem was the *separate condenser*. Steam was injected into the cylinder to push the piston up. Then a separate pump, worked by the motion of the beam, drew steam from below the piston into the condenser. Here it could be condensed with a jet of cold water. This created a vacuum in the cylinder and down plunged the piston into it. But the design differed from that of Newcomen's pump because Watt's cylinder remained hot all the time, ready to receive the next burst of steam. There was therefore no unnecessary waste of energy due to the alternate heating and cooling of the cylinder.

### John Roebuck

James Watt had an idea, but now he needed help. He turned first to *John Roebuck*, founder of a famous ironworks at Carron, near Falkirk. Roebuck wanted a more efficient engine to pump water from his nearby coal mine. He heard of Watt's ideas and undertook to build his engine in return for a two-thirds interest in his patent. But this engine was not a success; neither the workmanship nor the materials was good enough. When Roebuck ran into financial difficulties in 1773, he handed over his interest in Watt's engine to a new backer, Matthew Boulton.

### Matthew Boulton

Watt had first met Boulton in 1768. He had been impressed by his factory at Soho, Birmingham, where he produced buttons, buckles, sword hilts, clocks and other metal items. However, his rate of production depended on water power from Hockley brook, which often dried up in the summer months. So Boulton hoped that Watt's new engine would solve his own power problems at Soho, and he persuaded Watt to move to Birmingham. So began one of industry's most famous partnerships.

Because there would be no return on his investment for a good many years, Boulton extended the patent on Watt's invention for twenty-five years starting in 1775. Customers were supposed to pay an annual royalty for twenty-five years to the Boulton and Watt firm. This was to be one-third of the value of the coal saved by the new engine in comparison with a Newcomen pump.

The first Boulton and Watt engine was sold and started up in 1776, and twelve years later fifty-five were working. These first engines were only designed to give an up-and-down motion—like the Newcomen pump. Watt's next invention took a great step forward. He adapted his engines for

23. Newcomen's steam pump. When tap A was opened, steam at little more than atmospheric pressure passed into the cylinder. The counterweight of the pump rod helped to raise the piston—the idle stroke. Then tap A was closed and tap B opened, letting in a jet of cold water which condensed the steam in the cylinder, creating a vacuum. Atmospheric pressure then forced the piston down and so the pump piston rose, drawing water from the mine—the working stroke

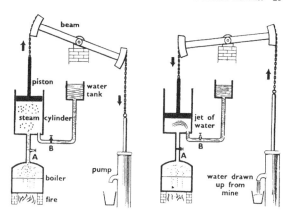

24. James Watt's improvements to Newcomen's steam pump

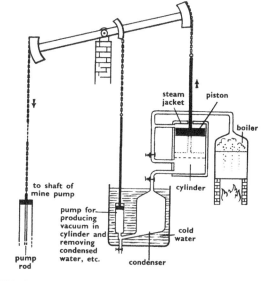

*rotary* (round-and-round) motion. In 1781 he patented his *sun and planet* gears; these enabled his engine to turn a wheel instead of merely pushing a piston. In 1782 he patented his *double acting engine*. Whereas Newcomen had used steam only on one side of the piston, Watt closed off the top end of the cylinder and used steam power to push his piston downwards as well. Thus Watt gained double the power for the same size of cylinder. Finally, in 1784 Watt patented a device he called *parallel motion*. The rotative, double-acting engine required a more rigid connection between the piston and the beam than the chains used on the Newcomen pump. To keep the piston rod moving in a

25. Watt's rotative beam engine, 1788 (Science Museum). Notice the large fly wheel, the sun-and-planet gear, the linkage (parallel motion) between beam and piston

straight line Watt devised a new system of linkage which he called parallel motion.

Boulton and Watt engines could now provide the reliable source of power that coal mines and factories, foundries and mills had been waiting for, and they soon came to be used for many other purposes. Breweries and distilleries used them; they worked the bellows in blast furnaces; Papplewick spinning mill, opened in 1785, was the first to be driven by steam. The engines pumped water out of tin and coal mines; they worked the hammers in forges. Watt's manager in Cornwall, William Murdock, invented a steam carriage in 1784; and soon the steam engine was to be adapted for use in steamships and steam locomotives. Moreover, because wood could not stand up to the vibration of a steam engine, the development of steam power brought about a dramatic growth in the use of iron (and later steel) in machine-making of all sorts.

### John Wilkinson
James Watt and Matthew Boulton cannot be given all the credit for the accurate engineering required for each steam engine. Only certain parts were actually made at the Soho works, for example valves, valve chests and valve gears. The other parts were made by outside firms, to whom Watt sent drawings and patterns. Notable among these was the firm of John Wilkinson of Broseley in Shropshire, which made nearly all the cylinders until Soho began to produce them in 1795. They called John 'Ironmad Wilkinson'. In 1774 he had launched the first iron ship on the Severn, a barge called *Trial*. He developed a more accurate method of boring the barrels of cannon; and he was even buried in an iron coffin! From boring cannon for the War Department it was but a short step to creating the cylinders required by Boulton and Watt. He showed his faith in the new engines by purchasing one in 1776 to pump the water that provided power for both his blast-furnace bellows and his forges.

# 5 Factory Conditions

Early factory machines were expensive and clumsy, but easy enough for a woman to work once they got started. Moreover, they could go on without stopping as long as workers could be found to tend and clean them. For cleaning, the smaller the worker the more easily he could get under the machines. So it came about that women and children were employed in great numbers, though men were still needed as 'overlookers', and for skilled, finer spinning.

Adults worked in the new mills for a variety of reasons. New methods of farming drove many workers from the land to seek employment in the towns. The ending of the Napoleonic Wars in 1815 caused a great reduction in the size of both the army and the navy. Wages were very low, and parents sent their children into the factories because they needed the money they earned. Moreover, they could lie about a child's age— compulsory registration of births was not brought in until 1836. The factories also employed orphans from the local parish workhouses. Poor Law authorities were only too pleased to get rid of their responsibility for these orphan children by apprenticing them to factory masters. So they were sent away and lived in grim 'prentice houses close to the mills.

Working conditions for both adults and children were, in most cases, appalling. Long hours were worked, generally 5 a.m. to 8 p.m., and when there was a rush of orders, this might be increased to 3 a.m. to 10 p.m. The children's work consisted mainly of cleaning the machines and tidying up, and simple repair jobs like tying broken threads. The idea was to allow the adults to work without having to stop. 'Piecers' tied broken threads together, 'doffers' changed the bobbins on the machines.

But the children had to work for hours in awkward positions; their limbs could become deformed; moving machinery could easily injure or kill them; and the great leather belts that transmitted power along the length of a building could cause terrible injuries if they snapped. The rooms in which people had to work were dirty, dark and hot; there were heavy fines for opening a window without permission; and women and children earned lower wages than men—in a normal week a child would earn 3 shillings (15p).

The following extracts, from a report prepared

26. A spinning room in a cotton mill, 1844. The child under the frame on the left is the *scavenger* picking up cotton waste

for Parliament in 1831, give a vivid picture of the lives of the children who worked in the textile mills.

### EVIDENCE OF SAMUEL COULSON

*'At what time in the morning, in the brisk time, did those girls go to the mills?'*

'In the brisk time, for about six weeks, they have gone at three o'clock in the morning, and ended at ten, or nearly half past at night.'

*'What intervals were allowed for rest or refreshment during those nineteen hours of labour?'*

'Breakfast a quarter of an hour, and dinner half an hour and drinking a quarter of an hour.'

*Was any of that time taken up in cleaning the machinery?'*

'They generally had to do what they call dry down; sometimes this took the whole of the time at breakfast or drinking, and they were to get their dinner or breakfast as they could; if not, it was brought home.'

*'Had you not great difficulty in awakening your children to this excessive labour?'*

'Yes, in the early time we had to take them up asleep and shake them, when we got them on the floor to dress them, before we could get them off to their work; but not so in the common hours.'

*'What time did you get them up in the morning?'*

'In general me or my mistress got up at two o'clock to dress them.'

*'So that they had not above four hours' sleep at this time?'*

'No, they had not.'

*'The common hours of labour were from six in the morning till half past eight at night?'*

'Yes.'

*'Did this excessive term of labour occasion much cruelty also?'*

'Yes, with being so very much fatigued the strap was very frequently used.'

*'Have any of your children been strapped?'*

'Yes, every one. The eldest daughter: I was up in Lancashire a fortnight, and when I got home I saw her shoulders, and I said, "Ann, what is the matter?" She said, "The overlooker has strapped me, but," she said, "do not go to the overlooker, for if you do we shall lose our work." I said I would not if she would tell me the truth as to what caused it. "Well," she said, "I will tell you, father." She says, "I was fettling the waste, and the girl I had been learning had got so perfect she could keep the side up till I could fettle the waste; the overlooker came round, and said, "What are you doing?" I said, "I am fettling while the other girl keeps the upper end up." He said, 'Drop it this minute.' She said, 'No, I must go on with this.'"

And because she did not do it, he took a strap, and beat her between the shoulders. My wife was out at the time, and when she came in she said her back was beat nearly to a jelly, and the rest of the girls encouraged her to go to Mrs Varley, and she went to her, and she rubbed it with a part of a glass of rum, and gave her an old silk handkerchief to cover the place with till it got well.'

*'What were the wages in the short hours?'*

'Three shillings a week each.'

*'When they wrought those very long hours, what did they get?'*

'Three shillings and sevenpence halfpenny.'

*'For all that additional labour they had only sevenpence halfpenny a week additional?'*

'No more.'

### EVIDENCE OF MR CHARLES STEWART

*'In which of Mr Boyack's mills are you employed?'*

'In a tow mill.'

*'The New Ward Mill, is it?'*

'Yes: there are fifty hands in the room altogether, old and young, and I found that out of that fifty there were nine who had entered the mill before they were nine years of age, who are now about thirteen years of age.'

*'Having been at that employment, then, four years?'*

'Yes, and out of those nine, there were six who were splay-footed, and three who were not; the three who were not splay-footed were worse upon their legs than those who were; and one was most remarkably bow-legged; she informed me she was perfectly straight before she entered the mills.'

Yet opinion at the beginning of the nineteenth century was against any change in the system. It was argued that children were safer in the mills than on the streets; that to use adult rather than child labour would increase costs, reduce demand and therefore cause unemployment; that living conditions were better in homes where children brought home a wage than in homes where they did not; and that to interfere in the relationship between a factory-owner and his workers was a crime against private property.

At first few Members of Parliament realised what was going on. They had little contact with the working class, and the art of collecting and using statistics was not known at the beginning of the nineteenth century.

## Some reformers

27. Michael Sadler

### Michael Sadler (1780–1835)

Michael Sadler was a Yorkshire MP who was horrified by the conditions in which children were working in the new cotton and woollen mills of Lancashire and Yorkshire. He became the leader in Parliament of those who were fighting for a reduction in working hours. He persuaded Parliament to appoint an official committee of inquiry, of which he himself became chairman. An election was held in 1832 before the committee had completed its work, and unfortunately Sadler lost his seat in Parliament. Although he died two years later, others carried on his fight.

### Richard Oastler (1789–1861)

Richard Oastler was a land agent in Huddersfield. It was a chance visit to a Bradford woollen mill that made him decide to fight for better working conditions for children. He drew attention to these conditions in a series of letters that he wrote to a newspaper, the *Leeds Mercury*, under the heading 'Yorkshire Slavery'. In one he wrote:

'Let truth speak out ... thousands of our fellow creatures, the miserable inhabitants of Yorkshire towns, are at this very moment existing in a state of slavery.... Would that I might rouse the hearts of the nation, and make every Briton swear these innocents shall be free.'

Oastler was one of those who worked hard to bring evidence about the children in the mills to the notice of Sadler's committee.

Later, because he could not pay some money that he owed his employer, he spent three years in a debtor's prison until his friends raised enough money to get him out. Even while in the Fleet Prison, he continued to write, urging that more should be done to reform conditions in the factories.

### Anthony Ashley Cooper, Lord Shaftesbury (1801–1885)

Anthony Ashley Cooper was also an MP. He sat in the House of Commons as Lord Ashley from

28. Anthony Ashley Cooper, Lord Shaftesbury

1826 until his father died in 1851. Then he became Earl of Shaftesbury and sat in the House of Lords.

When Sadler lost his seat in Parliament, it was Ashley who took up the lead in the struggle to improve factory conditions. Ashley wanted the factory day for everybody to be limited to ten hours. He argued that the State had an interest and right to watch over and provide for the moral and physical well-being of her people'.

Ashley had himself had an unsatisfactory childhood, with no real love and affection at home and grim experiences at school. Perhaps it was these events in his early life that made him determined to do something for the unhappy working children of the nineteenth century. He campaigned for factory reform, worked equally hard for the Coal Mines Bill (1842), and founded the Ragged Schools to provide education, food and clothing for the poorest of the poor. He became known as 'the children's friend'.

*Robert Owen (1771–1853)*
It must not be thought that all factories had a black record. There were some model employers, and one of the most outstanding was Robert Owen. Owen was a self-educated Welshman who trained as a draper's apprentice. By 1801, when he was thirty, he had become the managing partner of the spinning mills at New Lanark in Scotland.

When Robert Owen took over New Lanark it employed 2,000 workers, 400 of them children, some only five years old. He found drunkenness and thieving common, with families living in crowded, dirty rooms. Owen soon changed all this. He abolished child labour. He trained his adult workers well and set up schools for both them and the children. He shortened hours of work and went on paying workers when they were ill or on short time. He also built good houses for his workers, grew vegetables for them, and set up special shops where they could buy goods at cost price. It proved to be money well spent. His workers were contented, they worked hard, and therefore the mills prospered.

The world was astonished. New Lanark was visible proof that if you treated your workers well, they actually worked harder; that providing proper conditions for the workers did not bring ruin to the employers. People came from all over the world to visit the mills and see things for themselves, including the British Prime Minister and Grand Duke Nicholas, later Tsar of Russia.

### The factory acts: a summary
The activities of the reformers forced Parliament to introduce a whole series of laws dealing with factory conditions.

*The Health and Morals of Apprentices Act of 1802* limited working hours to twelve, with no night work. Children were to be given instruction in the three Rs. There was to be an inspection carried out by magistrates and clergymen. Since the local magistrates were very often also mill-owners the Act was not enforced.

*The Factory Act of 1819* forbade the use of children under nine, and limited the hours of older children. No effective inspection system was laid down, so this Act was not enforced either.

*The Factory Act of 1833* said that no children under the age of nine were to be allowed in factories. Children aged from nine to thirteen could work only nine hours a day; those from thirteen to eighteen could work twelve hours a day. Younger children were to work a shift system, so that in each day one and a half hours could be allowed for meals and two hours for education. Factories were to be open only from 5.30 a.m. to 8.30 p.m. To enforce these rules, full-time inspectors were appointed.

In 1840 a Royal Commission was set up to investigate the employment of children in general. Its report led to another *Factory Act* in 1844. This Act further limited working hours for children, and women were included in the regulations. Henceforth, there was to be no cleaning of moving machinery and fencing was to be put round the machines.

*The Ten Hours Act of 1847* was the work of *John Fielden* (Ashley had lost his seat in the House of Commons). A working day from 6 a.m. to 6 p.m., allowing for the time spent at meals, would mean ten hours' work for women and children. Meanwhile, adult male workers continued to work for longer hours and although textile factories had now been dealt with, other industries were not regulated at all.

Shaftesbury (formerly Ashley) continued his campaign. Acts in 1864 brought all child labour and most females too under Parliament's protection. This was particularly important for other industries, for example pottery, match-making, percussion cap and cartridge-making. As before, hours of work and age limits were laid down, and rules were to be enforced about ventilation and cleanliness.

Acts passed in 1867 made similar regulations first for all premises in which fifty or more people worked, and then for premises where fewer than fifty people were employed.

Finally, as far as we are concerned, the *Factories and Workshops Act of 1878* brought together in a single code all the rules about hours, ages, safety precautions, cleanliness, etc. The reformers were winning, but the war was by no means over yet.

# 6 Changes in the Towns

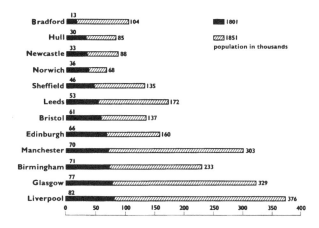

29. The growth of town population, 1800–51

| City | 1801 | 1851 |
|------|------|------|
| Bradford | 13 | 104 |
| Hull | 30 | 85 |
| Newcastle | 33 | 88 |
| Norwich | 36 | 68 |
| Sheffield | 46 | 135 |
| Leeds | 53 | 172 |
| Bristol | 61 | 137 |
| Edinburgh | 66 | 160 |
| Manchester | 70 | 303 |
| Birmingham | 71 | 233 |
| Glasgow | 77 | 329 |
| Liverpool | 82 | 376 |

■ 1801
▨ 1851
population in thousands

With the coming of steam power, factories could move from the banks of streams and rivers, which gave them water power, to towns that were near coalfields. At the same time, workers came in their hundreds to live near the factories because they preferred if possible to be near their place of work. As a result, small towns found themselves transformed into industrial cities far too quickly, without being able to do very much to influence the way this happened.

The population of England and Wales was going up rapidly anyway—from 9 million in 1801 to 21 million in 1851. London grew from 1 million people in 1801 to 2 million in 1841. Other towns increased in size even more rapidly (see the diagram).

Parliament made no regulations on overcrowding, standards of housing, fresh water, drainage, sewage, etc. There were no efficient local authorities with powers to regulate conditions in their own areas. Until the 1832 Reform Bill, many industrial cities had no representative in Parliament to draw attention to conditions. As a result, little could be done, and the problems grew worse.

## Overcrowding
There were no council houses in the nineteenth century. Houses were built too often by speculators eager to make a fortune. So too many buildings were crammed onto small sites, for example back-to-back dwellings, and the materials used and the standards of construction tended to be the cheapest.

Too often a house was rented by a tenant, who was then able to sublet the different floors or rooms; the tenant of a room might even then be able to sublet different beds within a room. Records reveal a room 4·5 metres by 3 metres in which lived 27 adults, 31 children and several dogs. In 1847, investigators in Church Lane, London, found, 1,095 people living in 27 houses. The pattern was the same in most industrial towns.

Even cellars were let as separate dwellings. At this time there were 15,000 people in Manchester living in cellars, and 39,000 in Liverpool.

## Refuse
There was no organised system of rubbish collection in these cities. People simply dumped their rubbish in heaps in the open, and since streets were not paved it was impossible to keep them clean. As there was no such thing as town planning, houses existed side-by-side with factories, workshops and even slaughter-houses. The flies, the rats, the filth

30. Back-to-back houses in Preston. Notice the privies draining into the open sewer between the houses

31. Court dwellings

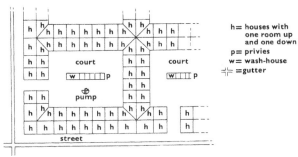

h = houses with one room up and one down
p = privies
w = wash-house
╬ = gutter

and the smell can well be imagined.

### Sewage

Sewage, likewise, was not disposed of in a safe, hygienic way, and houses did not usually have lavatories in them. Instead, two dozen or more families might share a set of privies—primitive sheds that had buckets or holes in the ground inside. Sewage was simply dumped in the street, or emptied into the nearest stream or river. Privies frequently became blocked and overflowed. There were, of course, no public lavatories in those days.

### Water

Fresh water was regarded as a luxury in the nine-teenth century and only the wealthy had it piped into their houses. The poor had to collect their water daily from pumps or taps in the street, and then store it. Water companies supplied it but, because the taps might be turned on only for an hour or two a day, the poor had to queue and often fight to obtain their water. Because it was so precious and obtained with such effort, it could seldom be spared for bathing and washing, let alone scrubbing.

### Fresh air

Even the circulation of fresh air was a problem. Narrow alleys and lanes do not make for good ventilation. Moreover, a short-sighted government introduced a Window Tax in 1808 to raise money.

32. A contemporary picture by Gustave Doré of Shaftesbury Avenue and Charing Cross Road, about 1850. There is a glimpse of the people who lived and worked in the cellars of the crowded houses

33. *A drop of London water* (*Punch*, 1850)

The result was that speculators were encouraged to put as few windows as possible into their jerry-built houses. This damaging piece of legislation was not repealed until 1851.

The poor could not take any action to put right this miserable state of affairs, the wealthy did not, and the speculators would not.

## The Municipal Reform Act, 1835

Some of the older towns and cities had, at various times in the past, been given a royal charter which provided for them to have a mayor and a corporation. However, few of these were elected by the people, and fewer still considered it their responsibility to do anything about the rapidly growing slums.

The *Municipal Reform Act of 1835* enabled the 178 towns that had charters to have councils elected by the ratepayers. Other towns could apply to have this right granted to them. The new councils could provide police forces and street lighting, and pave streets. But nothing was done to make them take any action over such things as sewers or drains.

From the 1830s better records were kept, and the publication of census figures and death rates helped. The facts could now be used to prove that living conditions in towns were bad enough to kill;

and that a child born in a town had only half as much chance of surviving as a child born in the country.

The population in general was also very ignorant about the causes of diseases and epidemics that attacked cities from time to time. Typhus, typhoid and, above all, cholera killed thousands, and yet few people saw a connection between poor living conditions and disease. The worst epidemics of cholera were in 1831–32, 1848–49, 1854–55 and 1865–66.

### Edwin Chadwick (1800–1890)

One man above all others led the campaign to bully the country towards better health. This was Edwin Chadwick who had already played a big part in reforming the Poor Law in 1834.

In 1842 Chadwick published his *Report on the Sanitary Conditions of the Labouring Population*. It revealed the shocking state of affairs that has already been described. The evidence of this report, together wth a serious outbreak of the dreaded cholera in 1848, which killed 55,000 people, convinced Parliament that it must intervene and take some sort of action.

The result was the passing of the *Public Health Act* in 1848. This Act set up a Central Board of Health, with Chadwick as one of its chief members. The Board had the power to compel a local authority to set up its own Board of Health; or if 10 per cent of the ratepayers in an area petitioned for a local Board the Central Board had the power to set one up.

About 200 boroughs used their new powers. But the others went on as before and the Act was dropped in 1854.

However, improvements had begun. Medical Officers of Health were appointed by progressive authorities; earthenware pipes were laid down to carry away sewage; and more cities began to get piped water supplies.

Other Acts of Parliament followed.

*The Common Lodging Houses Act (1853)* laid down standards of cleanliness and limited the number of people per house. The police were given powers to walk in and inspect premises.

*The Labouring Classes Dwelling Houses Act (1866)* allowed authorities to borrow money in order to build decent houses for labourers in overcrowded cities. Only Liverpool made use of the Act.

*The Housing Act of 1868* allowed a Medical Officer of Health to enter premises on his own initiative and to report unsatisfactory conditions to the local authority. If an owner refused to carry out improvements suggested by the local authority, the premises could be closed.

*The Local Government Act (1871)* set up the Local Government Board with a Minister of the government in charge. The whole country was divided up into Sanitary Districts.

*The Public Health Act of 1875* gave certain powers to those Sanitary Districts.

1. Undrained houses were to be fitted with drains, and all future houses must have drains.
2. All future houses were to be built with lavatories.
3. Cellar dwellings were to be controlled. No more were to be built.
4. There were powers to inspect and, if necessary, destroy unsound food.

*The Artisans Dwellings Act (1875)* allowed local authorities to begin slum clearance on a large scale. But only eleven cities tried to use the Act in its first ten years, and only Birmingham achieved very much. Under the energetic leadership of its mayor, Joseph Chamberlain, the city borrowed $1\frac{1}{2}$ million pounds, cleared factories and slums from forty acres, and then rebuilt both factories and homes in the suburbs.

The action taken by Parliament looks impressive on paper but was far less effective in practice. The problems of poverty, public health, and housing for the poor were immense. Much still needed to be done.

# 7 The Revolution in Communications

## Roads in the eighteenth century

'The country indeed remains in the utmost distress for want of good roads.' So wrote Daniel Defoe, the author of *Robinson Crusoe*, in 1724.

Since Roman times very little scientific road-building or mending had been done. An Act of Parliament of 1555 required local parishes to look after roads in their area. Farmers and landowners were to supply both the materials needed and the carts to carry them in. Local parishioners all had to work for six days a year without pay on road repairs. But these local workers were unskilled and uninterested, and a good standard was hard to enforce.

The roads were therefore very poor. In winter they were full of ruts and deep potholes, in the summer they gave off clouds of dust. In those days there were no obvious limits to the width of the road— no kerbs or hedges. So if a stretch of road was particularly dangerous, travellers simply found a way round it, and thus a new route was started.

Travelling was slow, painful and often dangerous. People travelled on horseback, sometimes making use of the system of post-horses. The travel-ler would change horses every 15 or 20 kilometres. He would have an attendant with him on each stage, who not only guarded him on the journey, but took charge of the horse when he changed over to the next. Goods travelled by pack-horse or slow-moving wagon. Teams of thirty or forty pack-horses travelled together, each capable of carrying about 100 kilograms in the two packs slung over its back. Unfortunately, they had the effect of churning up the mud even more as they passed. Sending goods by wagon was costly and slow.

There were some stagecoaches on the roads but the people who used them were lucky if they covered 15 to 20 kilometres in a day.

In the seventeenth century Parliament tried to preserve road surfaces by controlling the traffic that went on them. No hired wagon was to have wheels less than 11·16 centimetres wide or to have more than 7 horses, or to carry more than 1 tonne between 1 October and 1 May, or more than $1\frac{1}{2}$ tonnes during the rest of the year.

A more successful Act was the first Turnpike Act of 1663, and in the eighteenth century more and more turnpike trusts were set up.

34. A wagon, 1808. Notice the very broad wheels and the large team of horses needed before the new roads were made

## The turnpike trusts

A group of people woud get permission through a private Act of Parliament to take over a stretch of road—perhaps no more than 16 or 20 kilometres—and charge a toll to all users. The money raised by tolls would be used to repair and improve the road. At each end of a particular stretch of road, there would be a toll house and a gate, usually made of bars with spiked ends turning on a pivot, and therefore called a turnpike. Later the smaller trusts combined to form larger ones, but as late as 1830 there were over a thousand trusts controlling 35,000 kilometres of road.

The trusts could afford to pay a proper salary to hire an experienced road engineer to supervise their work. They were required not only to construct decent surfaces, but to build bridges where perhaps fords had been used, and to put up milestones at intervals.

Certain types of traffic did not have to pay toll, for example local farm traffic, crops being taken to barns, people going to and from church, and army officers and soldiers on the move. Coach companies usually paid a fixed annual sum to the turnpike trust. This meant there would be the least possible delay for their coaches at each gate.

Three men stand out as pioneers in the new art of road-building.

## John Metcalfe (1717–1810)

John Metcalfe, a Yorkshireman who had been blind since the age of six as a result of smallpox, came to be known as Blind Jack of Knaresborough. In spite of his blindness he engineered over 290 kilometres of improved roads across the moors and over the hills in the Pennine country of Yorkshire and Lancashire. He tested the road surface along his route by tapping away with his stick.

## Thomas Telford (1757–1834)

Thomas Telford was the son of a Scottish shepherd. As a young man he worked as a stonemason, as an architect, and then branched out into road and canal engineering. Appointed surveyor of public works in the county of Shropshire, he built roads, bridges, tunnels and canals. In 1802 he was appointed to examine means of communication in the Scottish Highlands. There he constructed some 1,480 kilometres of roads across difficult country and some 1,100 bridges. He built the Glasgow to Carlisle road, but his greatest achievement was the London to Holyhead road—the route to Ireland. This included Telford's famous suspension bridge (1826) over the Menai Straits, linking the Isle of Anglesey with the mainland of Wales.

Telford's roads were very solidly built but the great amount of materials they used made them very expensive. It was another road engineer, Macadam—also a Scot—who developed equally firm but much cheaper roads.

35. *The New Turnpike at Clifton Down*, Bristol. An early nineteenth-century picture. Toll houses had windows facing in each direction so that the keeper could watch the traffic

36. Telford's bridge over the Menai Straits. Notice the wide central span and the height of the bridge, which allowed tall ships to pass under it

37. Nineteenth-century improvements in road construction
Metcalfe: Flat subsoil. On this, a layer of broken stone and gravel. Camber on road surface. Drainage ditch either side

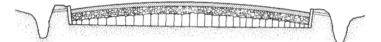

Telford: Level subsoil. On this, graded stone blocks. 15 cm of broken stone. Road surface 7·6 cm of gravel, cambered. Drainage ditch either side

Macadam: Cambered subsoil. 15 cm of stone chippings. Road surface 10 cm of gravel, cambered. Drainage ditch either side

*John Loudon Macadam* (*1756–1836*)
Macadam had been interested in the construction of roads since his schooldays.

From 1798 he began to build up a reputation as an engineer of roads in Cornwall. The methods he used there led to his appointment in 1815 as Sur-veyor-General to the Bristol Turnpike Trust, one of the biggest in the country. In 1827 he was made Surveyor-General of all roads in Great Britain.

Macadam did away with Telford's expensive foundations. He used simply layers of graded stones, which, under the weight of traffic, compressed into a road-bed almost as firm as concrete.

## Coaches

The new turnpike roads caused quite a revolution in travel. Goods and passengers could get to their destinations much more quickly. For example, in 1750 a journey from London to Edinburgh was reckoned to take 10 days; by 1830 this had been cut to 2 days. The travelling time from London to Holyhead had been cut from 3 days in 1785 to 27 hours in 1835. Now that road surfaces had become much more reliable, an increasing amount of travelling could be done at night.

Large coach companies sprang up to cater for the new traffic. One of the largest was Chaplin & Company, which in 1834 owned some 1,500 horses and 64 coaches. Although it was forbidden, coaches belonging to rival companies used to race each other along the new main roads. Controlling four horses required skill, and the coach drivers were held in great respect. When a coach was driven at speed the horses had to be changed every 48 kilometres or so, and the average working life of a horse on a fast coach was only four years.

Coaching inns were built in the towns where the coaches needed to stop to change horses. They provided rest and refreshment for weary travellers, and they might have stabling for hundreds of horses at the back. Where the timetable did not allow a lengthy stop, five minutes was the normal time allowed for the ostlers (grooms) to change the horses. Then the whip would crack and, with a creak and a jolt, the coach would be off again—with perhaps eight passengers inside and ten on top.

## The Royal Mail Service

Another development was the carrying of the mails by coach. It had been usual for letters to be carried by unarmed postboys, who travelled very slowly on horseback. A theatre manager from Bath called *John Palmer* used to travel a great deal up and down the road to London and he found himself overtaking his own letters. Deciding that this was not good enough, in 1784 he persuaded the government to use coaches for the mails. By the end of the century, eighty mail coaches left the General Post Office in London every day, carrying mail and passengers to all parts of the country.

38. A Royal Mail coach (Science Museum)

Nothing was allowed to delay the Royal Mail coach. At the turnpike it was allowed through without stopping. The keeper would rush out to open the gate as soon as he heard the coach's horn in the distance. Each coach, painted maroon and black, carried four passengers inside and four on top. The guard wore breeches and white stockings, a scarlet coat and a black hat, and carried: a sealed watch to keep an accurate account of his journey; a horn to warn inns and toll gates of their approach; a blunderbuss and a pair of pistols to ward off attacks by highwaymen; and an impressive tool kit to carry out repairs on the spot. If a serious accident occurred, the guard was expected to load the mailbags on to one of the horses and ride on. It was said that these coaches kept such good time that local people could tell the time of day by the Royal Mail clattering by.

Mail and stage-coaches could average up to 16 kilometres an hour and no road vehicles travelled faster than this until the motor car. But after 1830 the coming of the railways caused a rapid decline in coach travel. One after another the services came to an end. On 6 January 1846, the last mail coach drove into London.

## Canals

Better roads could not solve the problem of transporting heavy bulk materials, such as coal, stone, timber, corn, clay, sand, etc. Yet the Industrial Revolution meant that industry needed these materials and ways had to be found.

Much use was already made of sea and river transport. London, for example, got its 'sea coal' from Newcastle. But this was of little use to the industrial Midlands and Lancashire. Rivers very often did not flow where they were wanted. In any case, they tended to dry up in the summer months and ice up in the winter. If a mill or factory needed water power, a weir or dam was often built across the river in order to build up the flow of water. But this then hindered the passage of boats up and down the river.

People at that time did not believe that it was possible to build a complete artificial waterway, take it over natural obstacles like the Pennine hills and supply it with water. Short artificial cuts had been tried successfully here and there, however, in order to straighten out troublesome bends in a river, and it was only a short step to trying something more ambitious.

*James Brindley (1716–1772)*

Francis Egerton, third Duke of Bridgewater, had a problem. He owned some promising coal mines just outside Manchester at Worsley, but it was costing him far too much to transport the coal to Manchester. He had heard of the genius of a local man named *James Brindley* and he decided to ask him for a solution.

Brindley had started his career as an illiterate apprentice to a wheel- and millwright. In the 1750s, having set up his own firm, Brindley rebuilt the corn mill at Leek in Staffordshire. His reputation for solving problems, particularly any connected with water, earned him a nickname, 'The Schemer'. Between 1752 and 1756, Brindley was at work draining a coal mine at Clifton, also near Manchester, close to the home of the Duke of Bridgewater. He was an obvious person for the Duke to turn to for help.

Brindley planned a canal which would serve two purposes. Not only would it carry the Duke's coal to Manchester, it would also drain the mines at Worsley. Brindley's route started in tunnels right inside the coal mines, crossed the River Irwell by means of the Barton aqueduct, and finished in tunnels beneath Manchester. The canal was nearly 17 kilometres long and Brindley's skill made it level throughout; there was no need for any locks. It was opened in 1761.

The Bridgewater Canal in fact halved the cost of carrying coal to Manchester. It proved so successful that the Duke employed Brindley to extend it to join up with the River Mersey. When this extension was finished, raw cotton could be carried from Liverpool to Manchester at 30p a tonne instead of £2.

At first the canals were planned to serve local needs. But soon people began to see great possibilities in linking them to the rivers and joining them up to form a network. In particular, industrialists hoped to link up four great river systems—the Thames, Trent, Mersey and Severn—and to link each of them with the isolated but important city of Birmingham. Brindley by now was in great demand and had as many as six canal projects in hand at the same time. Much the most important was the Trent and Mersey or Grand Trunk Canal.

A famous manufacturer of pottery, *Josiah Wedgwood*, backed this particular canal. He needed china clay from Devon and Cornwall and flint from south-east England. He also needed some means of transporting his finished china away to the markets which did not cause expensive breakages. A canal

39. The Barton Aqueduct, built by Brindley over the River Irwell

seemed to be just what he wanted.

The Trent and Mersey Canal was an impressive achievement. In its 150 kilometres, it made use of 76 locks, 160 aqueducts, 213 road bridges and the 2,600-metre Harecastle tunnel. Brindley himself died before it was completed in 1777.

### The Canal Mania

In the early 1790s it seemed that everybody who had any money to invest hoped to get rich by backing canal projects. In the boom years 1791–94 it was called 'canal mania'. Some of the proposed canals could never be made to pay—they simply went from one unimportant place to another. Some were in agricultural areas where it was hard to make a profit because there were no industrial centres nearby. But many important canals were constructed:

*Rochdale Canal*, designed by *John Rennie*, crossed the Pennines.

*Huddersfield Canal*, designed by *Outram*, crossed the Pennines.

*Grand Junction Canal*, designed by *Thomas Telford*, linked the Thames and the Midlands. Finished 1805.

*Grand Union Canal*, designed by *John Rennie*, linked the Thames and Leicester. Finished 1810.

*Kennet and Avon Canal*, designed by *John Rennie*, linked Bath and Newbury. Finished 1810.

*Regent's Canal*, brought water transport into the heart of London. Opened 1820.

*Caledonian Canal*, designed by *Thomas Telford*, linked Inverness and Fort William in Scotland. Finished 1822.

### Construction of a canal

The promoters of a canal had to follow much the same procedure as the founders of the turnpike trusts. They formed a company in which people could invest money by buying shares, and they also had to put forward a private Act of Parliament. Having obtained permission from Parliament for their canal, they could set about buying up land along the chosen route and selecting an engineer to carry out the work.

The 'navvies' (navigators) employed to do the digging were a very tough gang. Many of them came from Ireland. They lived in huts and shacks alongside the works. They shifted great quantities of clay, rock and stone, drank great quantities of beer, and terrified local villages with their fights and violent behaviour.

The engineer had to work out the best line for his canal. He had to consider where his supplies of water were to come from, and whether to take the canal round a hill on the level, over a hill by means of locks, or through a hill by a tunnel.

Water was a key problem. Engineers usually built several large reservoirs at the summit level to maintain a steady supply, with perhaps a Boulton and Watt engine to pump the water into the canal. Most British canals were designed to be narrow in order to lessen this problem of water supply; unfortun-

40. The Grand Junction (now Grand Union) Canal at Apsley, Herts., about 1900, with narrow boats and a wide boat. The woman is leading the horse pulling the wide barge

ately, this was to lead to overcrowding later on. A lining of puddle clay about 45 centimetres thick along the sides and bottom of a canal bed prevented any water seeping out.

The canal companies owned the canals but not the barges; anyone could put a boat on a canal provided he paid for it. Most barges were worked by families who took a personal pride in the appearance of their boat and their horse. Both boats and utensils were skilfully decorated by hand, and at night it was the horse which was bedded down first in stables alongside the canal.

### Why the canals declined
One trouble with canals was that they could be put out of action so easily. Ice in the winter months could bring traffic to a standstill, until specially strengthened ice-boats pulled by as many as twenty horses arrived to force a way through. Sometimes a canal bank would slip, and water would pour out through the breach. All traffic had to halt while repairs were carried out.

Through traffic was very difficult because of differences in widths. A wide boat was generally 32·7 metres long and 5·25 metres wide, as against a narrow boat, which was 21 metres long and only 2·1 metres wide. Clearly a wide boat would not fit into the locks on a narrow canal. It was a pity that our narrow canals were not made double-tracked; instead occasional places were provided on most canals where there was room for two barges to pass each other. Sometimes, too, there were long delays

getting through locks; for instance, near Devizes there is a great staircase of twenty-nine locks to raise the Kennet and Avon Canal from the Vale of Pewsey onto Salisbury Plain. All in all, movement on a canal was a slow business for the normal cargo-carrying barge. Fly-boats were an exception. They carried parcels and sometimes passengers, were given double crews and permission to run all night and on Sunday if necessary, and used relays of horses to keep up a fast speed. A journey of 150 kilometres would take a fly-boat some forty-four hours, compared with a normal boat's four days.

Traders were dissatisfied with the amount of cargo stealing that took place during the course of a journey but, since there were as yet no regular police, this was not an easy problem to solve.

Canals were not able to adapt very easily to steam power when it came. Using an engine instead of a horse did not improve the average speed of the boats. Canal banks could not stand up to the wash that would be created by a boat travelling any faster. That is why most canals nowadays still have a 4 m.p.h. speed limit.

Railways, when they came, proved able to transport goods as cheaply as canal barges, and far more swiftly. To stop competition, the railway companies bought up many canals and then deliberately allowed them to decay. They diverted supplies of water, closed stretches of canals for supposed repairs, and used soft wood instead of hard when repairing fixtures like lock gates. In the 1830s there were about 6,500 kilometres of canal in a network across England; yet a mere forty years later it was obvious that most of them were doomed to be commercial failures.

## Railways

The idea of using rails on which to haul heavy loads goes back long before the coming of the railways. *Tramways* were much used in the mines: trucks of coal were hauled by men or horses on wooden rails from the mine to the nearest river or canal.

With the invention of the steam engine, it became possible to pull the trucks up quite a steep incline, using a stationary engine to wind in a cable attached to the trucks. In the north-east of England around Newcastle the trucks that were used by the coal mines happened to have an axle width of 4 feet

$8\frac{1}{2}$ inches (1·435 metres); their wheels were kept on the rails by a *flange*—a projecting rim on the rail.

Men began to think of making steam engines that could themselves run on the rails.

The first rails were made of wood and soon wore out. The next development was to cap them with iron. Then, as the quantity and quality of iron production improved, the engineers went over first to cast-iron rails and then to wrought-iron ones. The flange was kept on the rails in these early designs.

### Richard Trevithick (1771–1833)

One reason why Watt's steam engine could not be turned into a moving locomotive was that it was a low-pressure engine. The steam pressure used in the cylinder was little more than the atmospheric pressure of 15 pounds per square inch (1·05 kilo-

41. Rails and wheels: flange on the rail

flange on the wheel

42. Trevithick's Catch-me-who-can, Euston Sq., London, 1808

grams per square centimetre). It was felt that a higher pressure would lead to boiler explosions.

Richard Trevithick was the pioneer of high-pressure engines and the 'father' of the locomotive. In 1800 he made a winding engine for a Cornish tin mine with a steam pressure of as much as 50 pounds per square inch (3·5 kilograms per square centimetre). Then in 1804, he built one of his high pressure engines into a locomotive for Samuel Homfray, the owner of the Pen-y-Darran iron-works in South Wales. This engine pulled five wagons of coal and seventy passengers along nearly 15 kilometres of track to the Glamorganshire canal. Unfortunately, the cast-iron rails used by Trevithick broke under the weight.

In 1808 Trevithick's *Catch-me-who-can* created a sensation in London. This engine offered the public rides at a speed of about 20 kilometres an hour at a shilling (5p) a time, inside a circular enclosure near Euston Station.

In 1812 *Blenkinsop* designed an engine to pull loaded coal wagons from Middleton Colliery to Leeds. He gave his engine an extra driving wheel fitted with teeth, which engaged with cogs on the rails. It pulled twenty-seven wagons over a distance of 5·6 kilometres in an hour.

*William Hedley*, an engineer at Wylam Colliery near Newcastle, designed another famous loco-motive, the *Puffing Billy*, in 1813. By now it had been proved that the weight of an engine pressing down on a rail gave enough grip to the driving wheels. In addition, the flange had been transferred from the rail to the edge of each wheel, which was much less costly.

### George Stephenson (1781–1848)

It was George Stephenson, the most famous loco-motive builder of his day, who finally proved that steam power on rails could be made to pay.

Stephenson was born at Wylam, near Newcastle, the son of a fireman at the local colliery. At the age

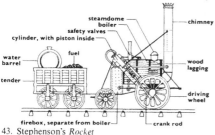

43. Stephenson's *Rocket*

of fourteen, not yet able to read, he got a job as an engineman. At eighteen he started night school in order to teach himself reading, writing and arith-metic. In 1804 he moved to another famous colliery, Killingworth, and continued to look after the vari-ous engines there. In 1814 he designed for Kill-ingworth a locomotive which he called *Blucher* after a famous Prussian general. Stephenson had married in 1802 and his son Robert showed just as much talent as an engineer. In 1824 father and son set up a famous locomotive-building firm at New-castle: Robert Stephenson & Company. Their engines were later exported to France, Russia, Ger-many, Italy and Belgium.

The year 1825 saw the opening of the Stockton to Darlington Railway. The railway company had chosen George Stephenson to design it and when the line was officially opened, the procession was headed by one of his engines, *Locomotion 1*. It hauled thirty-four coal wagons and one wagon filled with passengers. The line was intended mainly for goods traffic, and the emphasis was still on horse power rather than steam.

However, when it was proposed that a railway line should be built from Manchester to Liverpool, the directors of the company wanted to find the best method of pulling trucks and carriages. They de-cided to hold a competition on the Rainhill level, 14·5 kilometres from Liverpool. The directors offered a prize of £500 for the most reliable engine and laid down strict rules for the five competitors. The one horse-powered carriage and one of the steam locomotives managed to reach a speed of nearly 10 kilometres an hour. Two other steam locomotives broke down. But Stephenson's *Rocket* covered the track at an average speed of 22 kilo-metres an hour, reaching a top speed of 47 kilo-metres an hour. Steam power had won the day.

The design of the *Rocket* used a number of new features. As we know, steam provides the force which drives the pistons up and down inside the cylinders. One problem was how to heat the water inside the boiler quickly and efficiently even though the furnace had to be put at one end. The *Rocket*'s boiler had inside it twenty-five copper tubes each 7·62 centimetres in diameter. These conducted the furnace heat much more efficiently and transferred it to the water. The *Rocket* also had much better valves for controlling the amount of steam to the cylinders. Finally, Stephenson gave the *Rocket* the recently developed 'direct drive': the piston was directly connected to the driving wheel by a crank rod, without any gearing in between.

*Opposition to the railways*
The coming of the railways aroused a great deal of opposition—some of it laughable when we look at it 150 years later. People argued seriously that passengers in open carriages would be unable to breathe when travelling at such high speeds, and would be certainly suffocated in tunnels. Landowners complained that their estates would be split in two by the hideous embankments and cuttings, while farmers forecast that their cows would be so frightened by the noise and smoke of passing trains that they would cease to give milk.

Events proved most of the doubters wrong, as we shall see. However, turnpike trusts and canal companies complained loudly and correctly that they would be put out of business by the reliable, fast service offered by the railways.

*The Railway Builders: Robert Stephenson and Brunel*
*Robert Stephenson* (1803–59) made his reputation not only as a builder of locomotives but also as the designer of the famous London to Birmingham line. When the line was opened in 1838, it had cost more than 5 million pounds, and its 160 kilometres of double track had meant the construction of viaducts, bridges, cuttings, embankments and three tunnels. It was a colossal undertaking and good evidence of what the navvies could achieve.

Robert Stephenson was also concerned with two other main lines: London to Edinburgh, for which he built bridges over the rivers Tyne and Tweed, and London to Holyhead, for which he built his Britannia bridge (1850) over the Menai Straits.

*Isambard Kingdom Brunel* (1806–59) was also the son of a famous father; Marc Brunel was responsible for the first tunnel under the Thames, though he did not live to complete the task.

It was illness caused by the gases and fumes beneath the Thames that first brought the younger Brunel to Bristol in 1833. While he was recovering his health in the city he became involved in a proposed railway line between Bristol and London, and in the end was appointed its engineer. Parliament finally approved the plans for the line in 1835 but it had been a hard struggle. For eleven days Brunel had to withstand a tough cross-examination at Westminster by all sorts of opponents of the line, ranging from the Kennet and Avon Canal Company to the Headmaster of Eton, who was worried that his scholars would be disturbed.

Brunel had an original mind and was always prepared to take a fresh look at problems. It was typical of him to choose a 7 foot (2·1 metre) gauge for his Great Western Railway. After all, 4 feet 8½ inches (1·435 metres) had been the original choice simply because coal wagons in the north-east of England had happened to have that width of axle. Brunel now argued that a width of 7 feet would allow for much more powerful engines, giving greater speed and stability, and much more room for passengers. He won his point with his directors, even though the narrower gauge had already built up a substantial lead over him.

Brunel also improved the track on which his trains were to be run. Whereas the Stephensons laid their rails on stone blocks, Brunel preferred continuous lengths of pinewood with ties across the line at intervals of 4·5 metres to hold things in place. The Great Western Railway swiftly became famous for its smoothness, but the track cost over £300 a kilometre more than the traditional type.

The line was also famous for the high speeds it achieved. This was due partly to the directness of the route surveyed by Brunel, and partly to the genius of a young locomotive designer selected by Brunel, *Daniel Gooch*. He designed a series of powerful and reliable engines in the 1840s and 1850s, notable for 7 foot (2·1 metre) diameter driving wheels.

Brunel was also responsible for driving a famous tunnel through Box Hill to the east of Bath. It is reckoned that its construction used a tonne of gunpowder and a tonne of candles every week for two and a half years. Brunel also designed a famous station building at each end of his line: Temple Meads in Bristol and Paddington in London. The line was opened between London and Bristol in 1841 and extended to Exeter in 1844.

*Parliament intervenes*
Railways proved to be just as tempting to speculators as canals had been. In the ten years 1825–35, fifty-four Railway Acts were passed by Parliament, thirty-nine of them in 1836–37; and from 1844 to 1847 there was another series of boom years.

In 1844 Parliament passed an Act which influenced railway development even more drastically. The *Railway Passengers Act* (sometimes known as the Cheap Trains Act) compelled railway companies to carry third class passengers. Many, like the GWR, had refused to do so on the grounds that this would lower the tone of their railway, and that it was not in the country's interests for them to carry peasants, tramps, criminals and revolutionaries. The Act said that third class passengers

44. Box Tunnel on the Great Western Railway. Note the broad gauge engine coming out of the tunnel and the early signalling

must be carried in covered carriages at a charge of one penny per mile. Furthermore, companies were compelled to run at least one train a day in each direction along all their tracks.

Parliament was also faced with the problem of what to do about the two different widths of gauge being used in the country. Where the two met there was bound to be confusion. Goods had to be transferred from one size of train to another, and points systems outside stations had somehow to cope with different widths of track. By 1845, Brunel's broad gauge could boast 441 kilometres of track, mainly in the south, whereas the narrow gauge had a record of 3,060 kilometres of completed track, mainly in the north and Midlands. Trials were held between Darlington and York, and Didcot and Paddington, to see which trains performed better, and Brunel's GWR locomotive proved superior. However, the Royal Commission set up by Parliament to investigate the problem advised the country to adopt Stephenson's 4 feet 8½ inch gauge and this was done. In southern England, a third line was laid inside Brunel's track to accommodate narrow-gauge engines and coaches. This situation lasted until 1892 when on one dramatic day navvies ripped up the remaining wide track, and the last broad-gauge locomotives were driven to various depots and broken up.

### The effects of the railways

Railways undoubtedly changed the face of Britain. The gleaming metal rails sliced through the countryside; wooden and stone viaducts towered over peaceful valleys; stations like Euston in London meant the demolition of thousands of ordinary people's homes.

The railways created new towns where none existed before. Swindon, for instance, was chosen by Brunel and Gooch as a central base for their Great Western Railway. Locomotive building works were set up there and were in production by 1843. In addition, the directors decided to build a complete new town for their workers, with houses in six rectangular blocks, a church, a park and a library.

Newspapers and letters could be carried by the railways, and delivered more quickly than ever before. As a result, people living in places far away from London could be kept up to date with the country's news in a way not possible before.

Industry also benefited, for raw materials could be distributed and manufactures exported more speedily, cheaply and safely. Cities benefited because not only could they obtain food supplies more easily from local farmers, but many of their inhabitants could now move to the outskirts to live, and come in to work by train.

Railways, like turnpikes and canals before them, gave employment to vast numbers of people. In addition, the coal and iron industries were given a great boost by the increased demand for their products.

Railways enabled people to travel as never before. They came pouring into London on cheap excursions to gaze at the Great Exhibition in 1851. They began to take holidays in places like Brighton, Blackpool and Weston-super-Mare.

## Steamships

### *William Symington and the* Charlotte Dundas, *1802*

Steamships came before steam trains but their development was slower. Eighteenth-century inventors in France, Britain and America were all trying to apply steam to boats, and no one is quite sure who was the first to succeed. The American *John Fitch* got a steamboat going on the Delaware River as early as 1787, and went on to make five more.

In 1788 William Symington of Scotland made a little one-horsepower steamer which went at 8 kilometres an hour on a Scottish lake. In 1802, he did better still. With financial help from Lord Dundas, Governor of the Firth and Clyde Canal, he launched the *Charlotte Dundas* on that canal. Lord Dundas invited Symington to meet the Duke of Bridgewater, who at once ordered eight steamboats for his new canal.

Unfortunately, everything then went wrong for Symington. The Clyde Canal Company were worried that the banks of their canal would be damaged by the wash created by a steamboat, and they forbade the use of steamboats on it. The Duke of Bridgewater died and Symington lost the order

for boats on his canal. He himself died later in poverty.

### *Henry Bell and the* Comet, *1812*

Britain's first regular steamboat, the first commercial steamship in Europe, appeared on the Clyde. It was called the *Comet* and was built by Henry Bell. In addition to sails, it had a three-horsepower engine driving four paddle-wheels.

By 1823, there were more than a hundred steam vessels working on Britain's rivers, and many more in the United States.

### *Robert Fulton and the* Clermont, *1807*

Fulton, an American, had sailed on the *Charlotte Dundas*. Later he went to France to try to persuade Napoleon to use his new submarine *Nautilus* to invade Britain. While he was in France, he saw some plans of steamboats. On his return to America, Fulton ordered a boat 42 metres long and 4·8 metres wide, fitted with a Boulton and Watt engine.

In May 1807, the *Clermont* made her maiden voyage on the River Hudson from New York to Albany.

### *Crossing the Atlantic*

At that time, most people thought it would be quite impossible for a ship to cross the Atlantic Ocean under steam power, because no vessel could carry enough coal to keep the boilers going all the way.

45. The *Charlotte Dundas,* 1802

In 1819, the *Savannah*, an American sailing ship, crossed from Savannah to Liverpool in 27 days, 11 hours. She did use steam—she was fitted with paddles which could be lifted on board when the engines were not in use. However, she only used her engines for 85 hours out of the total time of 27 days.

There were of course technical problems to be solved. In those days most ships had wooden hulls, and wood did not easily stand up to the vibration caused by steam engines. The engines and the fuel that was needed to power them took up valuable space in the middle of a vessel and made a steamship less economic. Furnaces and boilers in a wooden ship involved too great a risk of fire, it was argued; and paddles were not really suitable for ocean crossings. If the ship rolled too much from side to side, one paddle-wheel would be almost clear of the water while the other was buried too deeply. Furthermore, paddle-wheels were too fragile to withstand the large waves created by Atlantic storms.

It was *Isambard Kingdom Brunel* of railway fame who took developments a stage further. In his mind he saw his Great Western Railway stretching beyond Bristol right across to America in the form of a steamship service. Casually he mentioned this idea at a meeting of railway directors; some of them took him at his word and formed the Great Western Steamship Company.

Brunel went on to design the *Great Western* to begin the service from Bristol to New York. She was a wooden paddle-steamer, 70·8 metres long and 10·5 metres wide. In 1838 she made a successful crossing to New York in 15 days, 5 hours.

The *Sirius*, a smaller ship chartered by a rival company, arrived in New York a few hours ahead of the *Great Western*. But she had started four days earlier, and had used up almost all her coal.

The *Great Western* established a fairly regular one-ship service across the Atlantic, making 67 crossings in 8 years. Her best times were 13 days westbound, and 12 days, 6 hours eastbound.

By now a screw propeller had been developed by both *Francis Smith* of Middlesex and a retired Swede living in England, *Captain Ericsson*. It was soon fitted to a suitable ship and in 1840 the screw-propelled *Archimedes* showed what she could do at Bristol. Two years earlier, an iron-built steamer, *Rainbow*, had also visited Bristol. Both vessels were examined by Brunel and their success guided him in the design of his next ship.

The *Great Britain* was also built at Bristol. Her design used a number of new features. Her hull was made up of metal plates riveted onto a sturdy metal frame of iron girders. She was given further internal strength to withstand a typical Atlantic battering by a series of bulkheads at intervals across the hull. Although she was fitted with short masts designed to carry a few sails, the *Great Britain* was designed with the new screw propeller. She was launched in 1843, and in 1845 made her maiden voyage to New York in 14 days, returning in 15½ days. Again she provided only a one-ship service; if at the end of a voyage she had to go into dock for repairs, passengers were expected to wait in nearby hotels.

### Samuel Cunard and the Royal Mail

So far, the only regular passenger services across

46. The *Great Britain*, 1843

47. The *Great Eastern*, 1858

the Atlantic had been provided by American companies—the Swallowtail Line, the Black Ball Line, the Red Star Line, etc. They operated fast, so-called clipper sailing ships, departing on regular advertised days of each month. They were able to do this because they used several ships, and they were able to charge high rates for both goods and passengers because their service was so reliable.

Samuel Cunard, a Canadian, saw the possibilities of steam power and planned a steamship service between Halifax, Boston and Liverpool. He won a contract to carry the mails for the British Government by offering a reliable four-ship service. In return, he received a subsidy of £81,000 a year to help maintain it. His four ships of identical size—Britannia, Acadia, Caledonia and Columbia—were built on the Clyde. In 1840 Britannia began the service for the British and North American Royal Mail Steam Packet Company. She crossed from Liverpool to Halifax in 14 days, 8 hours and returned in a mere 10 days. The company was later to change its name to the Cunard Company but continued its tradition of giving its ships names ending in the letters IA.

*Brunel and the* Great Eastern
Brunel's most ambitious venture was the steamship

*Great Eastern.* She was designed to be large enough to carry her own supplies of coal right round the world. Indeed, since she was 208 metres long there were only a few ports that could accept her. She was built with screw-propeller, paddle-wheels and sails. Her metal hull had not only the network of girders and the bulkheads that were such a success in the *Great Britain,* but also an inner, watertight metal skin. Her interior fittings were luxurious and included gas and electricity.

As usual, Brunel's ideas were far in advance of their time. The ship was so big that her launching into the Thames in 1858 had to be carried out sideways, something that had never been done before with a ship of that size. It proved to be a long-drawn-out process which ruined the finances of the company and ruined Brunel's health. He died the following year.

In 1860, the *Great Eastern* sailed to New York in $10\frac{1}{2}$ days and returned in $9\frac{1}{2}$. But she was never a commercial success because again she could provide only a one-ship service and never carried enough passengers or cargo to pay her way. Between 1865 and 1873 she did, however, have a much more successful career as a cable-laying ship.

# Suggestions for Further Reading

IRON
Ellacott, S. E., *Forge and Foundry* (Methuen Outlines, 1955)
Gale, W., *Iron and Steel* (Longman's Industrial Archaeology Series, 1969)
Trinder, B., *The Iron Bridge* (Ironbridge Gorge Museum Trust, 1973)
Trinder, B., *The Darbys of Coalbrookdale* (Phillimore, 1974)
Winton, W., *Iron and Steel* (an introduction to the iron and steel section of the Science Museum) (Contact Publications, n.d.)

SPINNING AND WEAVING
Ellacott, S. E., *Spinning and Weaving* (Methuen Outlines, 1956)
English, W., *The Textile Industry* (Longman's Industrial Archaeological Series, 1969)
Gilbert, K. R., *Textile Machinery*, Science Museum Illustrated Booklets (HMSO, 1971)
Hills, R., *Richard Arkwright and Cotton Spinning* (Priory Press, 1973)

Power, E. G., *A Textile Community in the Industrial Revolution* (Longman's Then and There Series, 1969)

COAL
Addy, J., *Coal and Iron Community in the Industrial Revolution* (Longman's Then and There Series, 1970)
Griffin, A. R., *Coal Mining* (Longman's Industrial Archaeology Series, 1971)
Tomalin, M., *Coal Mines and Mining* (Methuen Outlines, 1955)

WATER POWER AND STEAM POWER
Barton, D. B., *The Cornish Beam Engine* (Bradford Barton Ltd, 1965)
Cooper, L., *James Watt* (A. & C. Black, 1965)
Law, R. J., *The Steam Engine*, Science Museum booklet (HMSO, 1965)
Vialls, C., *Windmills and Watermills* (A. & C. Black, 1974)
Watkins, G., *The Stationary Steam Engine* (David & Charles, 1968)
Jackdaw no. 13, *James Watt and Steam Power* (Jackdaw Publications, 1965)

Printed and bound by CPI Group (UK) Ltd, Croydon, CR0 4YY
08/05/2025
01864433-0001